KERSPLASH!

A CLOUD BURSTS

Written by Jessica Kulekjian

Illustrated by Zoe Si

Kids Can Press

I am a cloud.

A
calm,
quiet
cloud.

I stretch into shapes as
I float in the sky,

and a thirst is swirling up inside.

Clouds give us clues about the weather. A big, puffy cloud can mean fair weather, but it can also mean a storm if the conditions are right. Better pack an umbrella, just in case.

I sip the steam from a cup of tea
and the spray from a garden hose.

I slurp up vapors from salty seas,
puddles and river flows.

Surge, gush, POUR!

Water freezes into ice that whirls in wild air, and with a crash, ice breaks.

DASH! An electric dance begins.

Lightning splits the sky.

CRACKLE!

STRIKE!

ZAP!

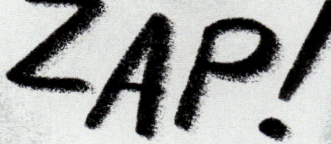

Soon, my thunderclaps go hush.
I'm frizzled,
drizzled,
drained.

Then, I fall back to the soil and return to the waters until ...
I rise to the sky again.

WATER CYCLE

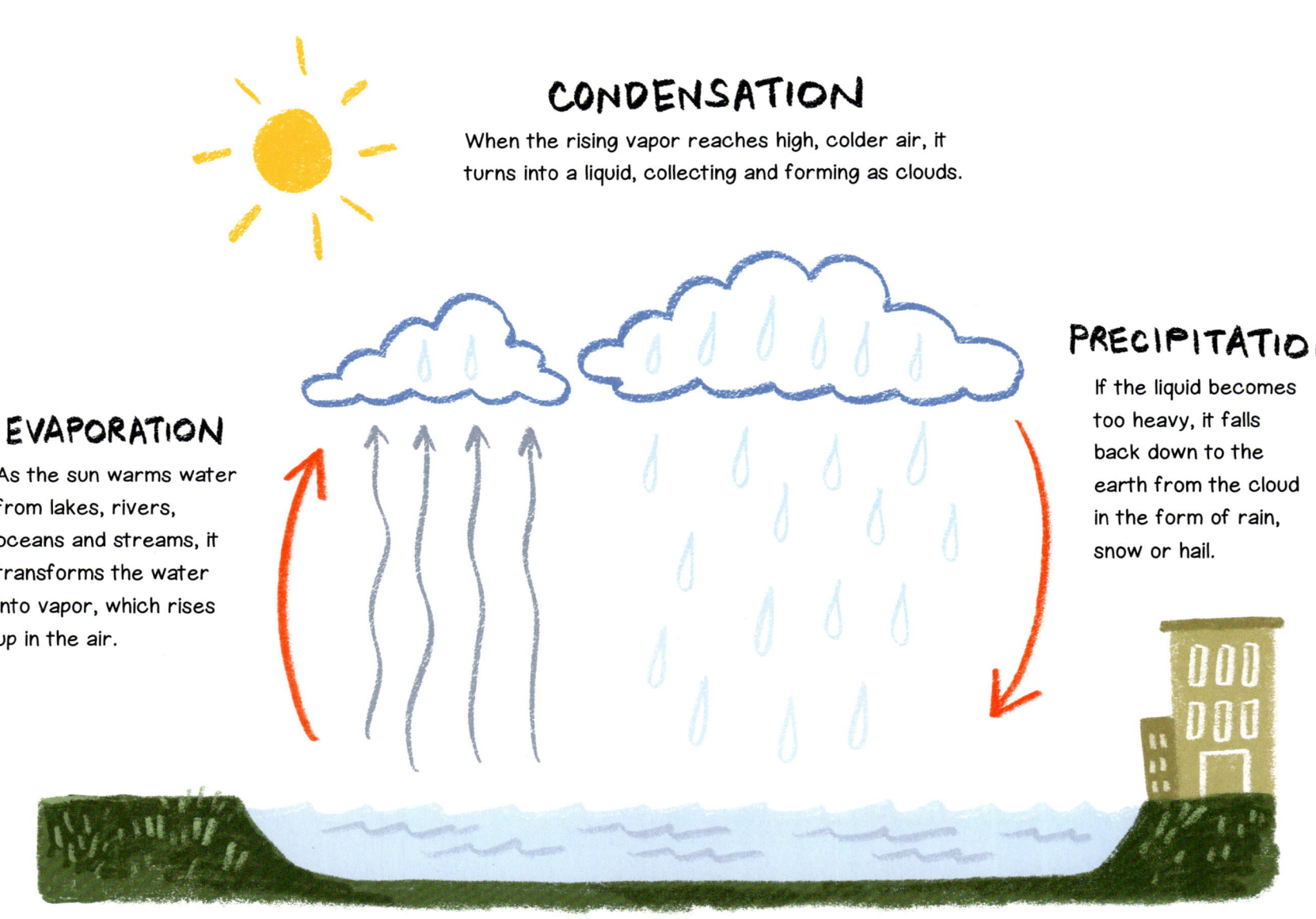

CONDENSATION

When the rising vapor reaches high, colder air, it turns into a liquid, collecting and forming as clouds.

PRECIPITATION

If the liquid becomes too heavy, it falls back down to the earth from the cloud in the form of rain, snow or hail.

EVAPORATION

As the sun warms water from lakes, rivers, oceans and streams, it transforms the water into vapor, which rises up in the air.

COMMON TYPES OF CLOUDS

Cumulus clouds look like puffy cotton balls. Their shape indicates what weather will follow. If they stay soft and white, it's not likely to rain. But, if they become tall and turn gray or dark, it's likely that a thunderstorm is coming.

Stratus clouds look like blankets that cover the sky. They usually mean it will be an overcast day, or that it will rain. If they are low to the ground, they are called fog.

Cirrus clouds look like wispy, thin feathers. They are located very high in the sky and can be a sign that rain or bad weather is coming. These types of clouds can arrive the day of or just hours before a storm.

There are many more types of clouds that are a combination of cumulus, stratus and cirrus. For example, **cumulonimbus clouds** are thunderstorm clouds (and the type featured in this book!). **Nimbostratus clouds** bring rain or snow. **Cirrostratus clouds** can create halos around the sun and moon.

LIFE CYCLE OF A THUNDERSTORM

Developing Stage (Cumulus Stage): As sunlight warms the earth, it heats the air, which causes the air to rise because warm air is lighter than cool air. As the warm air rises, along with water vapor and other particles — such as dust and salt — puffy clouds are created. The water vapor and particles continue to condense together into water droplets and ice crystals. If warm, moist air continues to rise, the clouds will continue to grow and change shape.

Mature Stage: As cumulus clouds grow, they become heavy from all the liquid they've absorbed, which darkens their appearance and changes their shape. Eventually, the warm air rising from the earth can no longer hold the water droplets in the cloud, so they fall with the help of air currents that move toward the ground. This is how it rains! Some water droplets freeze into ice crystals that whizz around inside the cloud. As the ice collides and breaks apart, electric charges are sparked, creating lightning and thunder.

Dissipating Stage: As the storm cloud drains of all its water, the air currents flowing down overpower the air that's flowing up. Since rising warm air cannot deliver more water into the cloud, the cloud shrinks, and the storm disappears.

Meteorologists — scientists who observe and study the weather — continue to learn more about the mysteries of storms and the sky. They share this information so everyone can know what to expect and how to prepare. What's the forecast in your neighborhood?

Author's Selected Sources

Books:

Fry, Juliane L. et al. *The Encyclopedia of Weather and Climate Change: A Complete Visual Guide*. Oakland, CA: University of California Press, 2010.

Kostigen, Thomas M. *Extreme Weather: Surviving Tornadoes, Sandstorms, Hailstorms, Blizzards, Hurricanes, and More!* Washington, D.C.: National Geographic Kids, 2014.

Lyon, George Ella. *All the Water in the World*. New York, NY: Atheneum/Richard Jackson Books, 2011.

Paul, Miranda. *Water Is Water: A Book About the Water Cycle*. New York, NY: Roaring Brook Press, 2015.

Yolen, Jane, and Heidi E. Y. Stemple. *I Am the Storm*. New York, NY: Rise, 2020.

Websites:

National Geographic. "Cloud." https://www.nationalgeographic.org/encyclopedia/cloud/.

National Severe Storms Laboratory of National Oceanic and Atmospheric Administration. "Severe Weather 101." https://www.nssl.noaa.gov/education/svrwx101/.

Sciencing. "Types of Clouds for Kids." https://sciencing.com/types-clouds-kids-8294039.html.

Videos:

National Geographic. "Thunderstorms 101." 2019. https://www.youtube.com/watch?v=zUNEFefftt8.

NOVA. "Earth From Space I Lightning Produces Nitrates." 2013. https://ca.pbslearningmedia.org/resource/nves.sci.earth.nitrate/lightning-produces-nitrates/.

For all those who look up with wonder at our shared sky — J.K.

For my parents, who made rainy Vancouver our home — Z.S.

ACKNOWLEDGMENTS

I'd like to thunderclap and shout out with gratitude to the following individuals for sharing their time and expertise to review and discuss the information found in this book. Thank you to Jennifer Dunn, Warning Coordination Meteorologist, National Weather Service, Fort Worth, Texas, and A.J. Fox, Certified Consulting Meteorologist, Certified Broadcast Meteorologist, Chief Meteorologist, KSEE24 Fresno, California.

Published in Canada and the U.S. by Kids Can Press Ltd.

25 Dockside Drive, Toronto, ON M5A 0B5

Kids Can Press is a Corus Entertainment Inc. company

www.kidscanpress.com

The artwork in this book was rendered in ink and watercolor, and finished digitally.
The text is set in GelPen.

Edited by Kathleen Keenan and Olga Kidisevic
Designed by Andrew Dupuis

Printed and bound in Buji, Shenzhen, China, in 10/2024 by WKT Company

CM 25 0 9 8 7 6 5 4 3 2 1

LIBRARY AND ARCHIVES CANADA CATALOGUING IN PUBLICATION

Title: Kersplash! : a cloud bursts / written by Jessica Kulekjian ; illustrated by Zoe Si.
Names: Kulekjian, Jessica, author. | Si, Zoe, illustrator.
Description: Includes bibliographical references.
Identifiers: Canadiana (print) 20240382307 | Canadiana (ebook) 20240382315 | ISBN 9781525308901 (hardcover) |
ISBN 9781525313684 (EPUB)
Subjects: LCSH: Hydrologic cycle — Juvenile literature. | LCSH: Clouds — Juvenile literature. |
LCSH: Rain and rainfall — Juvenile literature. | LCGFT: Instructional and educational works. | LCGFT: Picture books.
Classification: LCC GB848 .K85 2025 | DDC j551.48 — dc2

Kids Can Press gratefully acknowledges that the land on which our office is located is the traditional territory of many nations, including the Mississaugas of the Credit, the Anishnabeg, the Chippewa, the Haudenosaunee and the Wendat Peoples, and is now home to many diverse First Nations, Inuit and Métis Peoples.

We thank the Government of Ontario, through Ontario Creates and the Ontario Arts Council; the Canada Council for the Arts; and the Government of Canada, for their financial support of our publishing activity.